SOUND ENGINEER

Wil Mara

Published in the United States of America by Cherry Lake Publishing
Ann Arbor, Michigan
www.cherrylakepublishing.com

Content Adviser: Scott "Lance" McWhinney, sound engineer at the Michigan Theater in Ann Arbor, Michigan
Reading Adviser: Marla Conn, ReadAbility, Inc.

Photo Credits: ©Lijuan Guo/Shutterstock Images, cover, 1; © bikeriderlondon/Shutterstock Images, 5; © antb/ Shutterstock Images, 6; © Steve Wood/Shutterstock Images, 9; © Dragonimages | Dreamstime.com - Working In The Recording Studio Photo, 10; © Fuse/Thinkstock Images, 11, 21; © Dragon Images/Shutterstock Images, 12; © wellphoto/Shutterstock Images, 15, 17; © Ververidis | Dreamstime.com - A Mixing Console, Or Audio Mixer, shallow Dof Photo, 16; © Chyball | Dreamstime.com - Cat Photo, 18; © Nomadsoul1 | Dreamstime.com - Zombie Hand Coming Out Of His Grave Photo, 22; © nicolamargaret/iStock Images, 25; © track5/iStock Images, 26; © Bragikort | Dreamstime.com - Concert At Harpa Photo, 29

Library of Congress Cataloging-in-Publication Data

Mara, Wil, author.
    Sound engineer/Wil Mara.
        pages cm.—(Cool STEAM careers)
    Summary: "Readers will learn what it takes to succeed as a sound engineer. The book also explains the necessary educational steps, useful character traits, potential hazards, and daily job tasks related to this career. Sidebars include thought-provoking trivia. Questions in the backmatter ask for text-dependent analysis. Photos, a glossary, and additional resources are included."—Provided by publisher.
    Audience: Ages 8–12
    Audience: Grades 4 to 6
    Includes bibliographical references and index.
    ISBN 978-1-63362-563-1 (hardcover)—ISBN 978-1-63362-653-9 (pbk.)—ISBN 978-1-63362-743-7 (pdf)—ISBN 978-1-63362-833-5 (ebook)
    1. Sound engineers—Juvenile literature. 2. Acoustical engineering—Vocational guidance—Juvenile literature. 3. Sound—Recording and reproducing—Juvenile literature. I. Title. II. Series: 21st century skills library. Cool STEAM careers.

TA365.M364 2016
621.389'3—dc23
                                 2015005364

Cherry Lake Publishing would like to acknowledge the work of
the Partnership for 21st Century Skills. Please visit www.p21.org
for more information.

Printed in the United States of America
Corporate Graphics

ABOUT THE AUTHOR

Wil Mara is an award-winning and best-selling author of more than 150 books, many of which are educational titles for young readers. Further information about his work can be found at www.wilmara.com

TABLE OF CONTENTS

STEAM is the acronym for Science, Technology, Engineering, Arts, and Mathematics. In this book, you will read about how each of these study areas is connected to a career in sound engineering.

CHAPTER 1

A Passion for Noise

How would you like to be in the **studio** with a talented musical group as they record a new album? Or be at one of their concerts to help the band sound great live in a concert hall, and maybe even create a live recording? Maybe you want to work with voice artists to help make television commercials, bring cartoon characters to life, or create audiobooks. This is the kind of work that sound engineers do.

The job of a sound engineer involves skills in numerous areas that have to do with the science of noise!

Sound engineers help musicians record albums, but they do many other things as well.

Their work takes them into recording studios, live music venues, and even some surprising places to capture what we later hear on the radio, on television, on our iPods, and at the movies. The job requires a passion for noise.

While a carpenter works with saws and hammers, a sound engineer's "toolbox" includes such items as **microphones**, **speakers**, instruments, and **amplifiers**. The engineer has to know how this equipment functions inside and out, which requires a deep knowledge of technical details.

A console helps a sound engineer adjust the qualities of the sounds.

For example, a sound engineer must be able to master the large mixing **console** with its dozens of dials, meters, and inputs in order to precisely create the desired sounds. The engineer needs to know how to add more instruments to an existing song, creating one sound layer after another. This is called multitrack recording, and it is the standard today. The engineer also has to adjust the sounds that are already there. He might do this in the recording stage or the period afterward, which is often called the mixing stage. This process continues until the artist thinks that the beautiful sounds he hears in his head have been successfully captured for the world to enjoy.

Careers in sound engineering continue to grow as television, music, and radio markets expand. Besides recording studios, sound engineers work in stadiums, theaters, concert halls, churches, and many other venues around the world.

THINK ABOUT MATHEMATICS

Numbers play an important role in the world of sound engineering. As soon as you begin looking over the equipment, you'll start to see numbers everywhere—on the knobs, the meters, and sliders. Understanding how these numbers work together is critical for producing the best sound results. So take the time to learn the mathematics of the profession. Guessing will not be good enough!

CHAPTER 2

MASTERS OF SOUND

Today, most equipment is digital. But it wasn't that long ago that sounds were captured using reel-to-reel tape **recorders**. Each reel looked like a big wheel and had a long strip of recording tape wound around it. The various **tracks**—vocals, guitars, drums—were performed and recorded by the artists. Sometimes this happened all at once, sometimes one track at a time. This required long hours, many retakes, and an immense amount of patience. Today's computers make the process much easier, but it must still be guided by the artists making the recording and, of course, by the sound engineer.

Many sound engineers use both digital and analog equipment. "My gear at the Michigan Theater, for instance, has some digital **components**, but also a lot

Analog equipment is used to get a different sound and feel than digital equipment.

Many sound engineers work directly with musicians.

of analog components," says sound engineer Scott
"Lance" McWhinney. "The analog sound is to me
warmer and truer to the original sound created by a
person on stage. So while the industry has moved
toward digital in many ways, many of us appreciate
and stay with certain tried-and-true analog audio
components for their sound."

Many sound engineers have a fair amount of
musical talent. This can add even more creativity to the
process. In pop music, sound engineer Daniel Lanois

has won numerous awards for both his engineering accomplishments and his musical contributions. He's even played instruments on many of the recordings that he has also engineered. Artists like it when an engineer is also musical, as they know he will have a greater understanding of what they do. So if you have natural musical talent, don't be shy about developing it in your career as a sound engineer!

Someone with natural musical talent as well as technology skills might have promise as a sound engineer.

When recording music, sound engineers have to think about how the music will sound coming through earbuds.

Many engineers work to find the best way to deliver sounds through a car stereo, home stereo, or television speakers. But what about earbuds? Think of the challenge of recording a 90-piece orchestra in such a way that it sounds fantastic through a pair of massive speakers with a home entertainment system as well as a pair of headphones about the size of a marble. Now *there's* a mystery that only the best sound engineers can solve!

THINK ABOUT ART

Capturing sounds is an art form all its own. When it comes to working with the artists who actually create those sounds, there is a critical element to the sound engineer's job. She must have an appreciation for the sounds she's listening to, so that she can work with the artists to end up with the best product possible.

CHAPTER 3

POSSIBILITIES IN THE FIELD

When they're "in the field," meaning outside a studio, sound engineers sometimes face challenging circumstances.

One example of this is working at an outdoor concert with a live band. What if a thunderstorm occurs? The best sound engineer in the world can't eliminate all that background noise. Whatever the weather, the sound engineer has to determine where to put the amplifiers, microphones, and other devices. Then all of it needs to be wired together, which can mean miles of cables.

Some sound engineers mix outdoor concerts live, which can be challenging.

Once the equipment is set up, an engineer must oversee a process known as a sound check. This is done in order to get everything to sound perfect *before* the concert starts. The engineer balances the levels of all the instruments and vocals on the stage to create a musical blend that sounds good to everyone in the audience. The engineer also uses the console to take out any electronic whines, buzzes, or other unexpected noises.

During the concert, the engineer monitors the mixing board and makes small adjustments to assure that the

A good sound engineer is very familiar with his or her equipment.

audience gets the best sound possible. Sometimes, every concert in an entire tour will be recorded live. A sound engineer might also work at live theater performances.

A smart engineer knows that sound equipment is fragile and worth thousands, sometimes even millions, of dollars. Each piece needs to be packed up and moved carefully. A tour involves quickly setting up and taking down all the equipment, accounting for every piece, and boxing it to be moved. Then the process starts over in a new location. The sound engineer also may have to endure long plane rides, tiny hotel rooms, mediocre food, and extreme jet lag.

Radio and TV news reports sometimes require sound engineers to work in unsafe places, during severe weather conditions, or even at the sites of terrorist attacks. Sound engineers in the field have been badly injured or even killed, although this is rare.

Fortunately, most assignments with the news media aren't this dangerous. Radio, television, and Internet reports of all kinds require sound. The engineer may

Many sound engineers work in reporting, where they help conduct interviews.

A good sound engineer will take any assignment seriously, even if he has to record a cat meowing.

work at an Olympic event, or at a press conference from the White House. They may work at interviews with politicians, actors, and crime or accident victims.

Sound engineers are critical to television programs. They might work in the field on animal shows, even hanging from trees to record both the animals and the people talking about them. Sometimes a few sounds can transmit information to the viewer better than anything else!

In the field, a sound engineer might pack up some recording equipment—usually a digital recorder, some headphones, and a selection of microphones—and then go looking for the right sounds for the film that he or she is assigned to.

Sound samples taken from the real world are also used in video games. Think about all those explosions, tire squeals, audience cheers, and thunderclaps. A sound engineer went out and recorded those from real life. They may be "treated" in some way back in the studio for maximum effect. But sounds from the world around us can be just as interesting as anything created in a studio environment.

THINK ABOUT ENGINEERING

The basic aim of any engineer is to figure out how best to turn an abstract idea into a concrete thing. If the idea is to build a bridge, the engineer's job is to figure out how to correctly build it. Sound engineering is no different. Someone wants a certain sound, so the sound engineer's job is to figure out how to get it. To be successful at this, you need a vast storehouse of knowledge of the equipment you'll be using plus the creative talents to find new and effective ways to use it.

POSSIBILITIES IN THE STUDIO

If travel and possible danger don't sound appealing to you, don't worry—there are other sound engineering jobs that will suit you. Many sound engineers rarely work outside the studio environment. Some studios shoot weekly TV dramas, soap operas, or comedies. Other studios film news, cable talk shows, or early morning shows.

During the daily news shows, the engineer switches between commercials, live reports from the field, anchors reading the news from their desks, and taped features. The engineer checks the console and adjusts sound levels for

[21ST CENTURY SKILLS LIBRARY]

Sound engineers might need to switch back and forth between sources.

each segment. The job requires split-second timing, good physical coordination, and a great deal of knowledge about how a computer can capture the right sound. The goal is for the sounds from all these different sources to be heard clearly and at the same level. The engineer makes sure that listeners do not have to turn up the volume for one feature only to get blasted out of their seats during the next feature.

Nobody worried about sound in the early days of movies. Why? Because there wasn't any! Squeaky voices,

Scary movies need good special effects, and a sound engineer helps create them.

background noises such as cars and planes, and people coughing were not a problem. However, things changed drastically in 1927 when "talkies" arrived. Since then, sound engineers have played key roles in the creation of movies.

Creating all the right sounds for today's films is more demanding than ever. The engineer has to combine the voices of the actors, the sounds that are part of the action (doors opening, footsteps from another room, big explosions), and the music. As the engineer assembles all these elements, he has to make sure that they fit together perfectly. For example, if the music in one scene is too loud, it could distract the viewer from the storyline. On the other hand, if the horror film you're watching just had a terrifying moment, chances are that the action was accompanied by a blast of dramatic music that was very loud.

THINK ABOUT SCIENCE

The science involved in the capture of sound waves is fairly complex, but the best engineers take the time to learn it down to the tiniest detail. The study of sounds is known as **acoustics**, and you will unlock many mysteries of the sound engineering profession by learning as much about acoustics as you can. Many of the greatest sound engineers in history are experts at what others might think is boring technical stuff. The greater your depth of knowledge, the greater your chance of having a very successful career.

CHAPTER 5

BECOME A SOUND ENGINEER

As in most fields, there are personal characteristics that suggest a natural ability for working as a sound engineer. Having a good ear for sound is important. This is the ability to tell when an instrument is out of tune or something doesn't sound quite right. Learning to read music and play an instrument or two can be helpful.

A lot of home-recording technology is now available for anyone interested in becoming a sound engineer. As recently as the 1990s, musicians had to pay a small

Some aspiring sound engineers practice on equipment they keep at home.

Consoles are complicated, but a good teacher can help you understand how to use them.

fortune in order to get into a professional studio to make a recording. These days, you can purchase both software and hardware that you can hook up to a good computer to put together a home-recording setup. At the very least, you can download some basic multitrack recording programs and begin playing around with the features in order to understand what everything does.

Anyone can twirl knobs on a console, but only trained sound engineers can do it right. It's not so much how well you know the equipment but how well you can produce something with it. This is the ultimate measuring stick of a sound engineer's talents and abilities.

Employers who hire sound engineers will expect them to be trained beyond high school in several areas. These include advanced electronics, sound production and transmission, broadcasting, and computer technology. After a formal education, it is possible to get an **apprenticeship**. During this time, in return for lots

THINK ABOUT TECHNOLOGY

Sound technology is advancing all the time. Try to keep up, so that when you actually start your career, you will be familiar with the most up-to-date equipment. Same goes for recording and engineering software—it is constantly improving, but that also means it's becoming more and more complex. Those engineers who know how to use the latest software will be the ones who are in the greatest demand.

of work and fairly low pay, junior sound engineers can get on-the-job training from experts.

Another related career path you can take is one that improves and develops the technologies that help sound engineers do their job. Though it's more scientific in nature, those who can master sound technology and make contributions to the field can expect great rewards in return.

One perk of being a sound engineer is all
the great performances you get to watch!

THINK ABOUT IT

Watch a 30-minute animated TV show. As you watch, write a list of the sound effects you hear. Which sounds do you think the sound engineer had to invent? What do you think he or she used to create those sounds?

Sound engineers for news shows have to be very flexible with their schedules. They are often called to work on short notice. Why might this be true? Hint: Think of the times you see "Breaking News" on television.

Watch a live concert, an awards show, or a press conference on TV. Do you see sound engineers on the sides of the stage? Pay attention to what the event sounds like. Can you hear everyone's microphones? What do you think would be the best part of working as a sound engineer at this particular event? What would be the most challenging part? Why?

LEARN MORE

FURTHER READING

Brooks, Philip. *Radio*. Ann Arbor, MI: Cherry Lake Publishing, 2013.

Firth, Melissa. *Behind the Scenes at a Play*. New York City: Cavendish Square, 2014.

Kessler, Colleen. *A Project Guide to Sound*. Hockessin, DE: Mitchell Lane Publishers, 2011.

WEB SITES

Library of Congress—Audio Recordings
www.loc.gov/audio/?st=gallery
Check out this huge selection of interviews, songs, speeches, and other audio moments spanning hundreds of years in American history.

National Geographic Kids—Music Mixer
http://kids.nationalgeographic.com/games/more-games/music-mixer
Play this game to create your own rock band.

Rolling Stone—50 Greatest Live Acts Right Now
www.rollingstone.com/music/news/50-greatest-live-acts-right-now-20130731
Check out this list—with videos—of *Rolling Stone* magazine's ranking of the 50 singers and bands who put on the best live shows.

GLOSSARY

acoustics (ah-KOO-stix) a science that deals with the production, control, transmission, reception, and effects of sound

amplifiers (AM-pluh-fye-erz) devices that make sounds louder

apprenticeship (uh-PREN-tus-ship) a job that requires working for a set amount of time in return for instruction

components (kuhm-POH-nuhntz) parts of a larger whole, especially a machine or system

console (KAHN-sohl) panel of dials, levers, buttons, and switches that controls electronic equipment

microphones (MY-kruh-fohnz) instruments for magnifying sound electronically

recorders (ri-KOR-derz) devices that store sound for later playing

speakers (SPEE-kerz) devices used to transmit, or send out, sound

studio (STOO-dee-oh) room or building where movies, TV shows, and radio programs are produced

tracks (TRAKS) one of several songs or pieces of music on a musical recording

INDEX